Stewart J. Brown

AEC BUSES

SINCE 1955

Ian Allan
PUBLISHING

First published 2013

ISBN 978 0 7110 3651 2

© Ian Allan Publishing Ltd 2013

Published by Ian Allan Publishing Ltd, Hersham, Surrey KT12 4RG.

Printed in England

Visit the Ian Allan Publishing website at www.ianallanpublishing.com

Photographic credits
Every effort has been made to identify and correctly attribute photographic credits. Should any error have occurred this is entirely unintentional.

Contents

FRONT COVER Southampton Corporation was a major Regent V buyer in the 1960s, taking 70 – along with ten Swifts. Most of the Regents were bodied by East Lancs or the associated Neepsend business. This Neepsend-bodied bus was one of 25 delivered in 1964/5; they were 28ft-long 66-seaters with AV590 engines. Subsequent deliveries would be 30ft-long 70-seaters. From 1968 Southampton standardised on Leyland Atlanteans. *Ted Jones*

TITLE PAGE 1955 Reliance
East Kent took 40 Reliances with 41-seat Weymann bodies in 1955. One squeezes through an arch in Winchelsea on its way to Hastings in 1971. Later in the decade the Reliances would be joined by Regent Vs as East Kent turned to AEC as its main chassis supplier. *John Aldridge*

BACK COVER 1962 Reliance
Reading Corporation was an early user of standee single-deckers, initial orders being for AEC Reliances. Early vehicles were bodied by Burlingham, which by the time this bus was delivered in 1962 had been taken over by Duple and renamed Duple Northern. The bodies were of a style unique to Reading, with deep windows so that standing passengers could see out. They were dual-door 34-seaters. *Harry Hay*

Introduction

'Builders of London's Buses' was the proud boast of AEC. And it was true. The Associated Equipment Company had started life as the bus-building arm of the London General Omnibus Company in 1912 and became an independent business in 1933. The bulk of the buses being operated by London Transport in the middle years of the 20th century were supplied by AEC.

AEC built buses and trucks, and developed significant overseas business. It expanded in 1948 with the purchase of rival chassis makers Crossley and Maudslay. This led to the creation of Associated Commercial Vehicles as a parent company for the three chassis manufacturers, and in 1949 ACV purchased bodybuilder Park Royal and its recently acquired Roe subsidiary. ACV also acquired the truck-building interests of Thornycroft, in 1961.

There was rationalisation. Crossley, which built both chassis and bodies, was closed. The last Crossley DD42s – the company's main model – entered service in 1951, as did the last Maudslay Marathons. The last bodies to be built by Crossley were completed in 1958. Then in 1962 everything changed. The combining of ACV and Leyland was described as a merger, but it quickly became clear which of the two was the dominant partner – Leyland.

AEC's bus range carried on unchanged, and the two companies continued to compete for business. Thus AEC sold its Reliance and Regent in competition with Leyland's Leopard and Titan. Similarly the Swift, announced in 1964, competed with Leyland's Panther, even though the two models shared the same chassis frame. But AEC lost out through the lack of a model to compete with Leyland's Atlantean. AEC's involvement with London and the Routemaster saw it developing a rear-engined Routemaster as a potential Atlantean competitor – but that project was cancelled after the completion of just one prototype.

By the early 1970s AEC was, in the UK bus and coach market, a company with but one model: the Reliance. At the end of the decade there was much-needed rationalisation within the Leyland organisation, and that saw the closure of AEC's factory in 1979.

Stewart J. Brown
Hebden Bridge
April 2013

1962 Routemaster
'Builders of London's Buses' was for many years AEC's proud claim. And it was true. From the 1930s to the 1960s most of the buses purchased by London Transport were supplied by AEC. A Routemaster in Parliament Square makes the point as it hurries north to Camden Town. *Stewart J. Brown*

A varied range in changing times

In 1955 AEC was an interesting company with a range of exciting projects in hand. It was still building Regent III chassis, a model introduced in 1946 and being phased out in favour of the new Regent V. The last Regent IIIs entered service in 1956. The first two prototype Regent Vs had entered service in 1954, and production models were being delivered in large numbers from 1955. There were in essence two versions of the Regent V — a lighter-weight model with AEC's 7.7-litre AV470 engine, and a heavier-duty version powered by the A218 or, from 1959, the new AV590, both engines of 9.6-litre capacity. A small number of Regent Vs were built with Gardner 6LW engines in 1955/6. A long-wheelbase model was added in 1956, when the regulations on vehicle length were relaxed to allow the operation of two-axle 30ft-long double-deckers.

AEC was collaborating with London on a new model to succeed the RT and to replace the capital's 1,800-strong trolleybus fleet. The first Routemaster prototype was exhibited at the Commercial Motor Show in London's Earl's Court in 1954. There would be four prototypes in all, with series construction, by Park Royal, starting in 1959. There was another AEC integral too — the Bridgemaster, also produced in partnership with sister ACV company Park Royal. This was a low-height model, inspired by the Bristol Lodekka. A drop-centre rear axle allowed the Bridgemaster to be built to a height of just 13ft 6in with a central gangway on both decks. To achieve that height on a Regent V chassis required the use of lowbridge-style bodywork with the upper-deck gangway offset on the offside of the body.

1955 Regent III
Production of the Regent III was coming to a close in 1955. A late customer for the model was Carris, the provider of public transport services in Lisbon. This bus, still in regular service in 1979, had a Weymann body. The destination, Praça de Londres (or London Square), seems apt for such a British-looking bus — apart from the bumper which provided protection from Lisbon's erratic driving. *Stewart J. Brown*

The home-market single-deck range comprised two models. The Monocoach – a bus, despite the name – was another integral product built in conjunction with Park Royal. It had been introduced in 1953 but was found to offer no great benefits over the comparable Reliance chassis, and the last were built in 1957. The Scottish Bus Group was the biggest Monocoach user, taking 151 of the 190 supplied to UK fleets. The company's main single-deck model was the Reliance, introduced in 1953 to replace the heavy Regal IV. Both the Reliance and the Monocoach used AEC's horizontal AH410 6.75-litre or AH470 7.7-litre engine.

In the late 1950s the Regent V sold well, not just in the UK but in export markets too. It was a popular choice with companies in the BET group and was also bought by some of the biggest municipal fleets, including Glasgow, Leeds, Liverpool and Sheffield. The same cannot be said for the Bridgemaster. A forward-entrance model was added to the range in 1960, but when Bridgemaster production ended in 1963 just 180 had been built. The biggest buyer was the BET group, with 118.

The Reliance was also popular with BET operators, and with the Scottish Bus Group. It was bought by many independent operators too. The leading coachbuilders of the time – Burlingham, Duple, Harrington and Plaxton – all offered bodywork on the Reliance, and ACV tried with limited success to gain a share of this business by offering a Roe-built coach body, the Dalesman, on the Reliance.

Single-deck vehicles of up to 36ft in length were permitted on Britain's roads from 1961 (the previous limit had been 30ft), and AEC was quick to offer a long-wheelbase version of its Reliance, which was typically bodied as either a 49-seat coach or a 53-seat bus. It briefly offered air suspension, but there were few takers.

1955 Regent V
A minority of Regent Vs were fitted with exposed radiators. Among the operators choosing this option was Nottingham City Transport, which took 30 in 1955/6. They were D3RV models with 9.6-litre engines and vacuum brakes. They had 61-seat Park Royal bodies. When new they were predominantly green; this brighter livery was adopted in 1962. Nottingham's next AECs would be low-floor Renowns, in 1965. *Ted Jones*

1955 Regal IV
By 1955 most British AEC buyers had switched from the Regal IV to the Reliance. Cotter's of Glasgow took delivery of what was probably the last Regal IV coach to enter service in the UK, in the spring of 1955. The company was an early operator of Continental tours and perhaps thought the solidly built Regal IV offered a higher standard of comfort than the lightweight Reliance. It was a 9821S with 9.8-litre A219 engine and four-speed synchromesh gearbox and had a 38-seat Plaxton body. *Harry Hay*

1956 Monocoach

The Monocoach was developed as an integral ACV product using Reliance running units in a Park Royal body structure. The biggest UK buyer was the Scottish bus group, which had Monocoaches built by its main supplier, Alexander, as well as by Park Royal. The Alexander body resembled that built by Park Royal and used the same pillar spacing but had noticeably deeper windows, as comparison with the Park Royal-bodied Reliance on page 14 will reveal. This Alexander-bodied Monocoach was operated by Scottish Omnibuses and is seen in Airdie on a winter day. *Harry Hay*

1956 Regent V
Seven Regent Vs with East Lancs bodies joined the Eastbourne Corporation fleet in 1956 and set
the standard for the next seven years. Ultimately there would be 22 buses of this general style
in operation in Eastbourne, all with 9.6-litre engines. In the mid-1960s Eastbourne switched from
AECs to Leylands. *Ted Jones*

1956 Regent V

Rochdale Corporation bought its first Regents in 1935, and although it bought Daimlers too, AECs were the most common type in its fleet. It had 55 Regent Vs and these were delivered between 1956 and 1959. The first 40, which included this bus, were unusual in having Gardner 6LW engines, making them D2RA6G models, the '6G' at the end of chassis code indicating the use of the six-cylinder Gardner engine. The only other buyers of Gardner-engined Regent Vs were two Scottish municipals, Aberdeen and Glasgow. Rochdale's Regent Vs all had this style of Weymann body rather than the Orion, which by this time was in effect the manufacturer's standard. The Rochdale operation was taken over by SELNEC PTE in 1969. *Ted Jones*

1956 Regent V
In the 1950s Great Yarmouth Corporation bought AEC Regent Vs and Leyland Titans. In 1956
there were five Regent Vs with AV470 engines and bodies by Massey of Wigan. They seated 58.
By 1959 Great Yarmouth had 13 Regent Vs. *Ted Jones*

1956 Regent V
Maidstone & District bought large numbers of AEC Reliances but just one batch of Regent Vs,
22 entering service in 1956. They were AV470-engined MD3RV models with Park Royal bodies,
eight being of lowbridge layout, as here. These were M&D's last new half-cabs; the company was
an early convert to rear-engined double-deckers, first with Atlanteans and later with Fleetlines.
Omnicolour

1957 Bridgemaster
The Bridgemaster was launched in 1956, and the first four pre-production vehicles had stylish aluminium-framed Crossley bodies, as on this former demonstrator by now in the South Wales Transport fleet, seen carrying a respectable load on its way to Aberavon Beach, a few miles east of Swansea. Production buses had steel-framed Park Royal bodies which were rather less elegant.
Ted Jones

1957 Reliance
Between 1955 and 1969 all of the new single-deckers purchased by Aldershot & District were AEC Reliances. In 1957 it bought 30 with Weymann bodies, among them this example, seen outside Reading station in 1965. It would be withdrawn in 1970. *Harry Hay*

1958 Reliance
The most northerly customer for AEC was Highland Omnibuses, based in Inverness. It bought 33
Reliances between 1957 and 1962, including four delivered in 1958 which had 41-seat Park Royal
bodies. Similar vehicles were delivered to sister Scottish Bus Group companies Alexander's
and Scottish Omnibuses. *Stewart J. Brown*

1958 Reliance

Most of Douglas Corporation's new buses in the years after World War 2 were AECs, and most of these were double-deck Regents. But Douglas also bought a small number of single-deckers from AEC, including two Reliances with unusual Mulliner bodies. They were MU2RA models with Monocontrol semi-automatic transmission and were 7ft 6in wide – most Reliances were 8ft wide – and seated 42. They were still in service in 1976, when the Douglas operation was taken over by the new Isle of Man National Transport company. *John Aldridge*

1958 Regent V
In the 1950s West Bridgford Urban District Council ran just 28 buses, of which 25 were
AEC Regents. Three were delivered in 1958 and had rare double-deck bodywork by Reading
of Portsmouth. They were MD2RA models with AV470 engines and air brakes. *Omnicolour*

1958 Reliance
Baxter's of Airdrie generally bought AEC single-deckers and Leyland double-deckers. Burlingham
supplied Baxter's with both bus and coach bodies on Reliance chassis; this 45-seat bus was
one of seven generally similar vehicles delivered between 1957 and 1959. The Baxter's business
was bought by Scottish Omnibuses in 1962. *Harry Hay*

1959 Regent V

With the authorisation in 1956 of 30ft-long double-deckers many operators which adopted the new maximum length decided on forward-entrance bodywork. It was argued that there were benefits in having the entrance where the driver could keep an eye on it, because conductors were facing extra work as they collected fares from more passengers. East Kent was one of a number of BET operators to adopt forward entrances, starting with 40 Park Royal-bodied Regent Vs in 1959. This one is seen in Margate in 1975 in corporate NBC poppy red, and equipped for one-man operation – the clue is the box set in the radiator grille, which could be illuminated to advise intending passengers to pay as they entered. East Kent's stock of Regent Vs peaked at 161 buses.

John Aldridge

1959 Reliance

This style of Alexander bodywork was not commonly found on AEC chassis. The biggest user was Barton Transport, which took 18 between 1955 and 1960. This is a 1975 view in Sudbury, with the coach still in Barton colours but newly acquired by Rules Coaches of Boxford. The Plaxton-bodied coach on the far right is another Rules Reliance, which had been new in 1963 to Walls of Wigan.

Gavin Booth

1959 Regent V

From the purchase of its first motor bus, in 1950, to 1967 all of Ipswich Corporation's new buses were supplied by AEC. These included 60 Regents, all with AV590 engines and Monocontrol transmission. This is one of four delivered in 1959 which had attractive 65-seat Park Royal bodywork and was photographed in the town at a time when Adler was everyone's top typewriter. The lack of a rear-engined AEC double-decker saw Ipswich buying Atlanteans from 1968.

Stewart J. Brown

1959 Regent V
This style of Alexander body was supplied to all four Scottish municipal fleets in the late 1950s and early 1960s. In the Aberdeen fleet it was ordered on AEC and Daimler chassis, the former including five AV470-engined Regent Vs, although the AEC engines were soon replaced by Gardner 6LWs. *Harry Hay*

1959 Bridgemaster

The production steel-framed Park Royal Bridgemaster had a top-heavy look, although this could be lessened by an attractive livery, as on this King Alfred bus, one of a pair of rear-entrance B3RA models delivered in 1959. This is a 1973 view in the Broadway at Winchester, shortly before the King Alfred business was bought by Hants & Dorset. *Stewart J. Brown*

FACING PAGE

1959 Bridgemaster

In 1959/60 Southend Corporation purchased six Bridgemasters, all 30ft-long rear-entrance 76-seaters – a high carrying capacity for a front-engined bus. AEC had supplied most of Southend's motor buses from 1931, but the Bridgemasters were its last. They would be replaced in 1972 by one-man-operated Daimler Fleetlines. *Harry Hay*

1959 Reliance

David MacBrayne operated buses, lorries and ships which covered a large part of the west of
Scotland. From 1953 to 1970, when the business was absorbed by the Scottish Transport Group,
MacBrayne's big buses and coaches were supplied by AEC, while Bedfords were used where
smaller vehicles were needed. Reliance buses were employed on local services in Fort William and
included two with Roe bodies on Park Royal frames, delivered in 1959. The Fort William operations,
along with this Reliance, were taken over by Highland Omnibuses in 1970. *Harry Hay*

1960 Reliance
A unique style of Weymann coach body was supplied to Western Welsh on Reliance chassis in 1960 and 1961. This 1960 coach, complete with whitewall tyres, has been readied for the Brighton Coach Rally. *Glyn Bowen*

1960 Bridgemaster

The Bridgemaster was available in two lengths – 28ft and 30ft. The shorter model was chosen
by Grimsby-Cleethorpes Transport, this bus being one of four 66-seaters to enter service in 1960.
In the background an Austin FG van delivers Kodak film to a shop which, according to its window
display, also sells sun-tan lotions and cosmetics. *Ted Jones*

1960 Regent V
Traditional front-engined double-deckers rarely featured curved windscreens. Indeed, the only bodybuilder to use them was Northern Counties, on 12 bodies for Barton Transport and one for Southdown. The Barton buses were 11 Regent Vs and a Dennis Loline, and the end result was undeniably striking, as shown by this bus leaving Derby on its way to Nottingham. These buses were even more unusual in being lowbridge models with forward entrances – not a common combination. They were 70-seaters. *Stewart J. Brown collection*

1960 Regent V
In sharp contrast to the modern look of Barton's new Regents were 14 delivered to Leeds City
Transport. The only 30ft-long models to feature an exposed radiator, they were new in 1960
(the last year in which AEC built exposed-radiator Regent Vs) and had 71-seat Metro-Cammell
Orion bodywork. Leeds was the biggest UK buyer of AEC Regent Vs, taking 224. Pictured in 1999,
this bus is one of many Regent Vs to survive in preservation. *Ted Jones*

1960 Regent V
In the late 1950s and early 1960s Sheffield shared its orders between AEC and Leyland. AEC supplied 142 Regent Vs with bodywork by Alexander, Roe and, as on this bus, Weymann. To cope with Sheffield's hills the Regents were all powered by the larger AV590 engine. With the move to rear-engined buses Sheffield continued to buy Leylands – Atlanteans – but switched from AEC Regents to Daimler Fleetlines. *Stewart J. Brown*

1961 Reliance

Western Welsh was a major customer for AEC and in 1961 took ten Reliances with dual-purpose
Willowbrook bodies. Two are seen in Cardiff in 1963 during the Omnibus Society's presidential
weekend. E. L. Taylor, chairman of Western Welsh, was the Omnibus Society's president.
The moulding on the front panel was a feature of most Willowbrook bodies of this period.

Glyn Bowen

1961 Reliance
The Scottish Bus Group bought just over 600 Reliances between 1954 and 1966, the biggest user being Scottish Omnibuses, followed by Alexander's. Most SBG Reliances were bodied by Alexander, many with this style of 41-seat dual-purpose bodywork. Scottish Omnibuses was at this time Scotland's biggest AEC operator, running around 600 Regals, Regents, Monocoaches and Reliances. *Harry Hay*

FACING PAGE

1961 Regent V

For part of its tram-replacement fleet Glasgow Corporation ordered 89 30ft-long Regent Vs with 72-seat forward-entrance Alexander bodywork. In common with an earlier batch of Regent Vs for the city they featured a non-standard grille design. Delivery started at the end of 1960 and was completed in the spring of 1962. *Harry Hay*

ABOVE

1961 Regent V

South Wales Transport was a major customer for AEC, and its double-deck purchases in the late 1950s and early 1960s included Regent Vs, Bridgemasters and Renowns. The company was one of the biggest UK buyers of Regent Vs, with 214. Seen heading through Swansea is one of five delivered in 1961 with 71-seat Willowbrook bodywork. At this time the 350-strong fleet was 100% AEC. *John Aldridge*

Leyland takes over

Control of AEC and its associated companies within the ACV group effectively passed to its main rival, Leyland, when the two companies merged in 1962. But competition between the two companies continued, and new models appeared from AEC.

The Bridgemaster was replaced by a new low-frame chassis, the Renown, which could be fitted with bodywork by builders other than Park Royal. This was unveiled in 1962 and did rather better than the Bridgemaster, 251 having been built by the time production ended in 1967. As with the Bridgemaster, BET was a significant Renown buyer, taking 157. The problem with the Renown was that it was swimming against the tide. The Leyland Atlantean had been in production for over four years when the Renown was launched. The Daimler Fleetline had been around for nearly two. Double-deckers of the future would have their engines at the rear, not the front.

Indeed there were those who questioned whether the double-decker had a future at all at the start of the 1960s, as operators facing a steady decline in passenger numbers were looking at one-man-operated single-deckers as a way of cutting costs. A few operators ran Reliances as pay-as-you-enter buses with the driver collecting fares, but most operators wanted a vehicle with a better entrance than the three steps of the Reliance – a layout dictated by the high chassis frame.

AEC's answer was the rear-engined Swift. This used the same chassis frame as the contemporary Leyland Panther, but with AEC running gear. A number of municipal operators bought Swifts, but the really big buyer of the Swift was London Transport, which saw one-man-operated dual-door standee single-deckers as The Future. It wasn't. The Swifts had short lives in London.

Swift production ended in 1975. Sales were slowing following the legalisation of one-man-operated double-deckers, but the integral Leyland National was the final nail – or perhaps rivet – in the Swift's coffin.

Routemaster production continued apace in the early 1960s, but the only sales to operators other than London Transport were to Northern General, part of the BET group, and British European Airways. A rear-engined Routemaster was built for London in 1965 but remained unique.

One of AEC's healthy export markets was Portugal, where it worked closely with local manufacturer UTIC. This relationship saw a small number of AEC-engined UTIC integrals being imported to the UK in 1971/2, being sold as the Tagus. The UTICs followed another rear-engined model, the Sabre with a V8 engine. Only one prototype, with ECW body, was built for UK operation, in 1970.

The demise of the Swift and the abandoning of the Sabre left AEC with just one model for the UK, the Reliance. From 1968 this had been available for bodywork up to 12m (39ft 4in) long, following another relaxation of the length limits. Most 1970s Reliances were coaches, bodied by Duple and Plaxton – and, in smaller numbers, by European builders Jonckheere and Van Hool.

And then came the end. AEC's Southall factory closed in 1979. In an effort to retain the business of the independent operators which were by this time the main buyers of the Reliance, Leyland hurriedly engineered the installation of a ZF manual gearbox in the Leopard, hoping this would attract Reliance operators which might shun the Leopard's Pneumocyclic transmission. Some were convinced. Others objected to what they saw as Leyland's high-handed attitude and switched to imported chassis, mainly from Volvo – which would go on to buy the Leyland Bus business just eight years after the end of AEC.

FACING PAGE

1962 Renown

The low-height Renown was introduced in 1962 to replace the Bridgemaster. Whereas the Bridgemaster was an integral that used AEC running units in a Park Royal body structure, the Renown was a conventional chassis available to other bodybuilders. AEC built two demonstrators with Park Royal bodies, one being seen here with Edinburgh Corporation Transport – from which it failed to secure any orders. When its demonstration days were over it was sold to Burwell & District. *Harry Hay*

1962 Reliance

One of the earliest users of the 36ft-long version of the Reliance was Sheffield United Tours,
which took six with Plaxton Panorama bodywork in 1962. Coaches of this length typically
seated 49, but SUT specified just 44 seats to give its customers extra comfort. The horizontal
aluminium beading on the body side was a feature of SUT coaches in the 1950s and 1960s.
SUT was a BET subsidiary and after the creation of the National Bus Company became part
of National Travel North East in 1973. *Stewart J. Brown*

1962 Reliance

In 1962 Devon General bought nine Reliances with unusual Willowbrook Viscount bodies, for operation in its Grey Cars coach fleet. They were 41-seaters. Big side windows and glazed cove panels gave the company's patrons an excellent view of the Devon countryside.

Stewart J. Brown collection

1963 Reliance

Chesterfield Corporation was an early user of one-man-operated buses and in 1963 took six Reliances with 42-seat dual-door bodywork by Park Royal. Two doors were regarded by many urban operators as being necessary for successful one-man operation, as they allowed boarding passengers to get on without waiting for alighting passengers to get off. The 1963 buses had unusual single-letter reversed registrations; this 1978 view features 9027 R in Bakewell, operating on hire to Hulley's of Baslow. *John Aldridge*

1963 Regent V
Double-deck bodywork by Strachans of Hamble was rare indeed when this Regent V – one of
a pair – was delivered to A1 Service of Ardrossan. A 63-seater based on a 2D2RA chassis with
AV590 engine and Monocontrol semi-automatic transmission, it is seen passing through Irvine
on A1's main service from Ardrossan to Kilmarnock. *Harry Hay*

1964 Reliance
Glazed cove panels seem a bit of a luxury for a municipal bus in industrial South Wales but were
specified by Aberdare Urban District Council on a number of its buses, including two Willowbrook-
bodied Reliances in 1964. Between 1962 and 1971 all of Aberdare's new buses were supplied by
AEC, a mixture of Reliances and Swifts. The Reliances – there were 23 of them – had dual-door
bodywork. *Stewart J. Brown*

1964 Reliance
A more luxurious Welsh Reliance was this coach operated by Jones of Aberbeeg – a Harrington Grenadier on a 2MU4RA chassis with AH470 engine and constant-mesh gearbox. Jones took four Harringtons in 1964/5, the other three being on Leyland Leopard chassis. The Jones business was bought by NBC in 1969. *Stewart J. Brown*

1964 Reliance

Scottish Omnibuses had standardised on the AEC Reliance for its single-deck fleet and generally chose small rather than large engines. Thus in 1964 it was buying 36ft Reliances with 7.7-litre AH470 engines. All of the company's long Reliances had Alexander Y-type bodies; this coach seen in Gifford was a 49-seater. *Gavin Booth*

1964 Reliance
Timpson's was a substantial London coach operator, running 100 vehicles and generally buying AEC Reliances. It was quick to switch to 36ft coaches. This Reliance with 49-seat Plaxton Panorama body was one of four identical coaches delivered in 1964. Timpson's was owned jointly by the BET and Tilling groups and disappeared in 1973 when under NBC control it was amalgamated with Samuelsons to form National Travel South East. *Stewart J. Brown*

1964 Regent V
Blue Ensign of Doncaster bought two new Regent Vs. This one was delivered in 1964 and had a
73-seat Roe body. It is seen in 1974 looking as good as new as it leaves Doncaster's south bus
station. The coach-style polished wheel trims were an unusual feature for a double-deck bus and
are indicative of the care taken by Blue Ensign in the presentation of its buses. The two Regent
Vs were replaced in 1975 by a pair of Daimler Fleetlines. *John Aldridge*

1964 Regent V
Another Doncaster operator, Felix, also took a 73-seat Roe-bodied Regent V in 1964 but specified conventional rear-entrance bodywork. Felix had eight Regent Vs, all with rear-entrance Roe bodies. Six were still in use when the company was bought by the South Yorkshire PTE in 1976 but were withdrawn the following year. *John Aldridge*

1964 Reliance

From 1955 until the end of production in 1979 most of the new coaches purchased by Yelloway
Motor Services of Rochdale were AEC Reliances. The company switched to 36ft-long models in
1962, but with just 45 seats instead of the 49 more commonly specified for the new generation
of longer coaches. Those supplied between 1961 and 1965 had Harrington bodies; when Harrington
closed Yelloway switched to Plaxton. *Stewart J. Brown collection*

1964 Regent V
Douglas Corporation ran 43 buses when three Regent Vs were delivered with forward-entrance Willowbrook bodies – the first double-deckers of this layout on the Isle of Man. The Corporation's first double-deckers, in 1933, had been Regents, and apart from three wartime Daimlers – with AEC engines – every double-decker bought by Douglas was an AEC Regent, 38 in all, over 35 years, which meant that in the 1950s and 1960s new Regents were replacing old ones. *Ted Jones*

1965 Renown

BET subsidiary East Yorkshire Motor Services operated 50 Bridgemasters, purchased between 1960 and 1963, and then progressed to the Renown, taking 34, all with Park Royal bodies, between 1964 and 1966. They were the company's last new front-engined buses; subsequent deliveries would be Daimler Fleetlines. This is Beverley in 1974. *John Aldridge*

1965 Renown

Apart from one batch of Dennis Lolines all of the double-deck buses bought by City of Oxford Motor Services from 1930 were supplied by AEC. There were Regents, Bridgemasters and, last of the line, Renowns. There were 43 Renowns in the Oxford fleet (making the company the biggest operator of the model), most of them bodied by Park Royal. The last were delivered in 1967. The company's next new double-deckers were Daimler Fleetlines. *Ted Jones*

1965 Reliance
Most of the single-deckers in the Maidstone & District fleet in 1965 were AEC Reliances, and
in that year a further 20 were delivered, fitted with standard BET-style 53-seat bodies built by
Weymann. M&D's livery, complete with cream flash below the windscreen, made the body look
rather less utilitarian than the plainer liveries used by some other companies in the BET group.
Note the hub covers on the rear wheels. *John Aldridge*

1965 Reliance

London Transport bought one batch of Reliances, which were fitted with BET-style Willowbrook bodies. There were 14 coaches in the RC class, and they had a chequered history on Green Line coach services because of their poor reliability. Built as 49-seaters, in 1969 they were downseated to 43 and fitted with luggage racks and were briefly allocated to route 727, which linked Luton, Heathrow and Gatwick airports, as seen here in Reigate in 1970. The route board above the side windows is a feature of the 1930s rather than the 1960s. Most of the RC-class Reliances ended up on local bus services. *John Aldridge*

FACING PAGE AND ABOVE

1965 Reliance

The availability of the AH590 engine in the 36ft-long Reliance from 1961 was a response to improvements in the road network which saw operators looking for vehicles suitable for sustained running at relatively high speeds over long distances. Two 36ft-long 2U3RA Reliances joined the fleet of Dodds of Troon in 1964 and had Duple Continental bodies with a higher floor level than was normal at the time. The Continental name was apt for this coach, seen on tour in Paris. Note how bright the interior is compared with modern coaches, thanks to the glazed cove panels and the generous provision of roof lights. In 1979 the pair were fitted with rather less stylish Willowbrook bodies, following which they were operated by Dodds for five more years; the same coach is seen after rebodying, at a rather less glamorous location – Leith Links – in 1981.

Stewart J. Brown, Gavin Booth

FACING PAGE

1965 Routemaster

The only buyer of Routemasters outside London was BET's Northern General Transport company, which took 50 in 1964/5. They were 30ft-long forward-entrance buses with 72 seats and Leyland engines. NGT later acquired the only other Routemaster of this specification, which had been built as London Transport RMF1254 but was never operated by LT. *John Aldridge*

ABOVE

1965 Regent V

Between 1958 and 1968 Garelochhead Coach Services bought six new AV470-engined Regent Vs, and these were used mainly on the company's service between its home town and Helensburgh. Four of the Regents had forward-entrance Northern Counties bodies with unusually small destination displays. *Harry Hay*

1965 Routemaster

London Transport introduced two batches of Routemaster coaches to its Green Line operations, in 1962 and 1965. The 1965 RCL-class vehicles were 30ft long and seated 65, compared with 72 on a standard 30ft Routemaster bus. As well as having coach seats the Green Line RCLs had AV690 engines and a high-ratio rear axle. Although still in London Transport green, this RCL was in the ownership of London Country and had been downgraded to bus work when photographed leaving West Croydon bus station in 1973, at which time a Golden Rover provided a day's travel for 75p. *Stewart J. Brown*

1966 Reliance

Small operators were generally slow to adopt 36ft-long single-deckers for bus operation following the legislative change (in 1961) that permitted their operation. One exception was Gillett Bros of Quarrington Hill, which took a couple of long Reliances in 1963 and added another four in 1965/6; all had Plaxton bodies. A 1966 bus in Hartlepool shows the use of short bays on early 36ft-long Derwent bodies. Gillett Bros did buy a few Bedfords, but the majority of its vehicles came from AEC. The company was bought by United Automobile in 1974. *Stewart J. Brown*

1966 Reliance
In 1966 City of Oxford Motor Services added a pair of 36ft-long 6MU3R Reliances to its small
coach fleet, replacing 14-year-old Regal IVs. They had 45-seat Duple Commander bodies,
built in the former Burlingham factory in Blackpool. *Harry Hay*

1966 Reliance
Most Alexander Y-type bodies for Scottish Bus Group companies were on Leyland Leopard chassis, but between 1963 and 1966 there were 237 Y-type Reliances for the three Alexander's companies and Scottish Omnibuses. The last of those for Scottish Omnibuses were 36ft-long 2U3RA models with AH590 engines and ZF gearboxes. These proved troublesome on intensive inter-urban services, and 16 were transferred to Highland Omnibuses in 1969, to be followed by six more in 1973. Two are seen on town services in Inverness in 1974. These were SBG's last new AECs. *John Aldridge*

1966 Reliance
Maidstone & District was a regular customer for Reliances and in 1966 took ten 36ft models
with 49-seat dual-purpose Marshall bodies. These used the standard BET bus shell but with
high-backed seats, a chrome grille and bumper, and twin headlamps. One manœuvres in London's
Victoria Coach Station prior to departing for Sheerness. M&D had taken near-identical Weymann-
bodied Reliances in 1965. *Stewart J. Brown*

1966 Reliance
Aldershot & District took 12 Reliances with Metro-Cammell 49-seat bodies in 1966. Pictured
in Farnham in 1968, one shows the simplified fleetname adopted by A&D the previous year.
John Aldridge

1966 Reliance

Two Willowbrook-bodied Reliances joined the fleet of Pontypridd Urban District Council in 1966 and were followed by two more in 1967. They had 45 seats. By this time Willowbrook was offering the option of the BET-style curved windscreen, but Pontypridd stayed with the less expensive option of flat glass for its Reliances. Pontypridd's was a small fleet, with 50 buses, but the undertaking was a regular buyer of AECs, taking 26 Reliances and Regents between the delivery of its first 1961 and its last 1972. Although exhorting customers to pay as they enter, the bus in this 1974 view is carrying a conductor. The ornate shaded fleet number harks back to an earlier era. *Stewart J. Brown*

1966 Routemaster
The AEC-Park Royal Routemaster was London Transport's standard double-decker from 1959 to 1967. Later vehicles were all 30ft-long 72-seaters, easily identifiable by the short bay amidships. The Routemaster proved to be incredibly long-lived, the last examples not being withdrawn from mainstream service in London until 2005. *Stewart J. Brown*

1966 Swift
Garelochhead Coach Services was buying Regent V double-deckers in the 1960s, when
it evaluated this Swift demonstrator. Bodied by Marshall, it was the second and last Swift
demonstrator. *Harry Hay*

1966 Swift

City of Oxford was one of AEC's most loyal customers, buying little else until the days of the
National Bus Company. In 1966 it took eight Swifts with 53-seat Willowbrook bodies. MP2R
models with AH505 engines, they were the first Swifts for a BET-group company; the only
other BET buyers of the rear-engined AEC model were East Kent, East Midland and South Wales.
Freshly repainted in NBC's corporate poppy red, one pulls out of Reading's gloomy bus station
in 1973, heading back to its home city. *Stewart J. Brown*

1966 Routemaster

The great might-have-been. AEC built just one rear-engined double-decker, Routemaster FRM1.
It was supplied to London Transport and operated on various routes, first in Central London,
then in the Croydon area and finally at Potters Bar, before being allocated to the Round London
Sightseeing Tour, as seen here in 1979. It was withdrawn in 1983. It's easy to snipe at Leyland for
pulling the plug on a model which would have competed with its Atlantean, but ten years after the
launch of the original front-engined Routemaster AEC had found just one buyer outside London
(Northern General), so there was no reason to believe that the rear-engined version would do
any better. Indeed, Leyland was to learn precisely that lesson in the late 1970s when its Titan,
designed for London, found few takers anywhere else. *Stewart J. Brown*

1966 Regent V
Devon General was buying both Regent Vs and Leyland Atlanteans in the 1960s. The last Regents were five with 59-seat Metro-Cammell bodies delivered in 1966, which took to 91 the number of Regent Vs in the 300-vehicle fleet. One is seen in Newton Abbot bus station in the National Bus Company's corporate poppy-red livery. *Ted Jones*

1967 Swift

Wolverhampton Corporation placed just three orders with AEC, for three Reliances in 1963, five Renowns in 1966 and finally for six Swifts in 1967. The Swifts had dual-door 54-seat Strachans bodywork and were the fleet's first rear-engined buses; Wolverhampton was at this time still buying front-engined Guy Arab double-deckers. The Swifts – and six similarly bodied Roadliners which came at the same time – were its last new buses. In 1969 Wolverhampton's operations were taken over by the newly created West Midlands PTE, and this bus, still in its original livery, is seen in PTE ownership in 1973. *Stewart J. Brown*

1967 Routemaster
The buses used by British European Airways to transfer passengers between Central London and Heathrow Airport were managed on BEA's behalf by London Transport – which explains the choice of Routemasters for a new BEA fleet in 1966/7. There were 65, and they were the only short forward-entrance Routemasters. When new they were blue and white; this red livery was adopted in 1970 – and would in turn be replaced by another blue and white scheme when BEA was merged with BOAC in 1974 to create British Airways. A trailer was provided for passengers' luggage.
Stewart J. Brown

1967 Swift

Morecambe & Heysham Corporation took half-a-dozen Swifts in 1967, and these were the undertaking's first one-man-operated buses. The 50-seat bodywork was built by Seddon's Pennine Coachcraft business. They marked a turning-point in the operation, which at the time of their delivery was entirely double-deck. No more double-deckers would join the fleet. Four more Swifts were purchased, following which Morecambe & Heysham switched to Seddon Pennines. Under the reorganisation of local government in 1974 Morecambe & Heysham was absorbed by neighbouring Lancaster. *Stewart J. Brown collection*

1968 Swift

In the mid-1960s the Sheffield Transport fleet was made up mainly of double-deckers, but in the latter half of the decade, in common with many other urban operators, Sheffield introduced one-man-operated single-deckers, in the form of 22 Park Royal-bodied AEC Swifts. As in many other places, the Swifts would be its last AECs. Double-deckers continued to dominate in the Sheffield Transport fleet, and these would be supplied by Leyland and Daimler. *Stewart J. Brown*

1968 Swift

The biggest order for Swifts in Wales came from Cardiff Corporation, which took 20 with Alexander W-type bodies. They were dual-door 47-seaters with space for 16 standing passengers. Cardiff specified a non-standard front end with flat windscreens; the standard W-type body had a rather more stylish frontal appearance with curved windscreens and a complex glass-fibre moulding, as shown on page 84. *Stewart J. Brown*

1969 Swift

The Swift was available with a choice of two engines – the 8.2-litre AH505 and the 11.3-litre AH691. There had been a plan to build a heavy-duty export model which would have been called the Merlin (both the swift and the merlin are birds), but this never materialised. However, London Transport adopted the Merlin name for its 36ft-long AH691-engined Swifts, taking 665. Their lives in London were generally short, the longest-lived being the Metro-Cammell-bodied buses used on Red Arrow limited-stop services in Central London, which survived until replaced in 1981 by Leyland National 2s. Here one heads down Park Lane in 1979. *Stewart J. Brown*

1969 Swift

Nottingham City Transport was primarily a double-deck fleet, but in 1969 six Swifts were purchased. They had dual-door 43-seat bodywork by Northern Counties. The Swifts had relatively short lives in Nottingham, being sold in 1975 to Grimsby-Cleethorpes Transport. *Stewart J. Brown*

1969 Swift
Most of Portsmouth Corporation's buses were Leylands when nine AEC Swifts were delivered in 1969. They had dual-door 42-seat bodywork by Marshall and followed a batch of Leyland Panther Cubs, suggesting some dissatisfaction with the Leyland model. Portsmouth had last bought an AEC in 1931. That the Swifts might not have been a glowing success either is suggested by the subsequent purchase of single-deck Leyland Atlanteans. *Stewart J. Brown*

1969 Kudu

For export markets AEC produced front-engined chassis right up to the end of production at Southall. On the Ranger the engine was above the front axle, but for South Africa there was an alternative model, the Kudu, which retained the vertical AV590 engine but had the axle set back to provide an entrance opposite the driver. On most Rangers and Kudus the bodybuilder incorporated AEC's standard radiator grille. This bus was in the fleet of Benoni Town Council. The kudu is an African antelope; the oval badge below the AEC lettering on the grill features an outline of the animal's head. *Stewart J. Brown*

1970 Sabre
At the 1970 Commercial Motor Show at London's Earl's Court AEC exhibited this coach, the only
Sabre to operate in Britain. It was ahead of its time, with a rear-mounted 247bhp 12.1-litre V8
engine – at a time when the most powerful Reliance was rated at 157bhp. Bodywork was by ECW.
It was sold to Best's of Ealing but by the end of the 1970s was running for Kemp's of Nonington,
Kent. The badging below the illuminated front panel reads 'Leyland Sabre'. *Stewart J. Brown*

1970 Swift

Surely the most unusual Swifts were three with Sparshatt bodies, delivered to the British Overseas Airways Corporation in 1970. The body layout gave a whole new meaning to the term front entrance, with its forward-facing loading platform. The Swifts had 35 seats, doors on both sides, and could carry a further 35 standing passengers. BOAC was merged with British European Airways in 1974 to create British Airways, in whose ownership this bus is seen at London's Heathrow Airport in 1978.
Stewart J. Brown

ABOVE

1970 Swift

Blackpool Corporation's bus fleet at the close of the 1960s was made up entirely of Leyland Titans, so an order for AEC Swifts came as something of a surprise. There first 15 entered service at the start of 1970, and follow-on orders took the fleet to 55 by 1974. All were MP2R models, with AH505 engines and Monocontrol transmission, and they had 47-seat dual-door bodywork by Marshall. After the Swifts Blackpool went back to Leyland, taking long-wheelbase Atlanteans. *Stewart J. Brown*

FACING PAGE TOP

1971 Swift

The biggest buyer of rear-engined AECs was London Transport, which ordered 1,503. Most were delivered in the period 1968-71 as part of the organisation's grand Bus Reshaping Plan, whereby high-capacity standee single-deckers were to usher in a bright new age for London's bus users. It was a failure. The buses were short-lived and brought to an ignominious end the long association between AEC and London Transport. This 33ft-long Swift in Croydon was bodied by Park Royal and had 33 seats, with room for 34 standees. An advertisement on the side encourages would-be passengers to tender the exact fare. *Stewart J. Brown*

FACING PAGE BOTTOM

1971 Swift

The Country Area operations of London Transport were taken over by the National Bus Company in 1970, and early deliveries to the newly formed London Country Bus Services included 138 Swifts which had been ordered by LT. Also seen in Croydon, this bus has a Metro-Cammell body with 41 seats. It was licensed to carry 19 standing passengers. *Stewart J. Brown*

1971 Reliance

In the winter of 1971/2 there was a significant change to the Green Line fleet operated by London
Country Bus Services with the delivery of 90 AEC Reliances bodied by Park Royal. The bodywork
was of a style unique to London Country, featuring a bus shell, coach seats and a front windscreen
which was the same as that used on the company's Park Royal-bodied Leyland Atlanteans. These
new coaches were delivered in dark green but were soon repainted in NBC local-coach livery, as
seen here at Harlow bus station. Note, however, how NBC's corporate 'double N' logo fails to hide
the origins of a sign designed to display London Country's short-lived wheel-and-wings device.

John Aldridge

1972 UTIC integral

In the early 1970s the Moseley coach dealership imported a small number of Portuguese-built UTIC integrals which featured AEC running units. Just nine were sold, Bonas of Coventry being the biggest user, with three. They were 53-seaters and had a rear-mounted AH691 engine and a six-speed ZF gearbox. Moseley named the coach the Tagus, after the principal river in Portugal.

Stewart J. Brown

1972 Reliance

Dodds of Troon, a member of the AA Motor Services co-operative, bought small numbers of new Reliances. These included two delivered in 1972 which had Willowbrook Expressway bodywork – a style not often found on heavy-duty chassis. They were 49-seaters and were operated until 1986. Here passengers board an Ayr-bound coach in Ardrossan in 1982. *Stewart J. Brown*

1972 (1962) Reliance
Between 1972 and 1974 East Kent had new Plaxton Panorama Elite bodywork fitted to 30 of its early 36ft-long Reliances. The Plaxton bodies replaced originals built by Park Royal and gave the 10-year-old coaches a new – and more luxurious – lease of life. This coach has a 1962 chassis and a 1972 body. *Stewart J. Brown*

1972 Swift

Among the more unusual coaches operated on Green Line services were 21 Swifts with Alexander W-type bodies. The W-type was normally a bus, but the vehicles delivered to London Country had 45 high-backed coach seats. They had been ordered by South Wales Transport. The Alexander-bodied Swifts were short-lived, being withdrawn in 1977/8. Here one loads in Reigate for a day tour in 1972. *John Aldridge*

1972 Swift

Great Yarmouth Corporation took 11 Swifts with dual-door Marshall bodies in 1972. The operator had bought Regent Vs in the late 1950s and one batch of Reliances in the mid-1960s. It returned to AEC as a major supplier in 1970, when it received its first Swifts. By the end of 1973, when the last were delivered, it was running 33. *Stewart J. Brown*

1973 Swift

In the 1960s Lowestoft Corporation's small fleet – comprising just 15 buses – was made up
entirely of double-deckers. However, when a major fleet replacement programme was implemented
from 1969, it switched to single-deckers, choosing AEC Swifts with bodies built in the town by
Eastern Coach Works. There were ten in all, and they were dual-door 45-seaters. This one is seen
in 1977, following local-government reorganisation (in 1974) which saw Lowestoft Corporation
succeeded by Waveney District Council; there was no change to the bus livery. Later in 1977
the operation, though not the buses, would be taken over by Eastern Counties. *Stewart J. Brown*

1973 Swift

Inspired by city-bus operation in Continental Europe, Sunderland Corporation stopped buying double-deckers in the mid-1960s and instead standardised on dual-door standee single-deckers. Most of these were Leyland Panthers, but Sunderland also ordered two batches of AEC Swifts, of which ten were received in 1968, and a further 18 delivered to the town in 1973 after its bus operations had been taken over by Tyneside PTE. This is a 1973 bus, seen in the ownership of Tyne & Wear PTE in 1978.

Stewart J. Brown

1976 Reliance
Eight Reliances with 49-seat Willowbrook Spacecar bodies joined the National Travel South East fleet
in 1976, one being seen four years later with National Travel London, loading for a tour. The Spacecar,
launched in 1974, was Willowbrook's attempt to challenge the established luxury coachbuilders but
was not a resounding success. From 1973 until the end of production the Reliance was powered by
the 12.4-litre AH760 engine. *Stewart J. Brown*

1976 Reliance
Left-hand-drive coaches with British registrations are rare indeed. Four left-hand-drive Reliances, 6U3ZL models, were supplied to National Travel South East in 1976 for operation on services to Continental Europe, an Athens-bound coach being seen in London's Victoria Coach Station in the summer of 1979. The long exposure has blurred the motion of the driver who is loading the roof-mounted luggage rack – a strange anachronism on a 1970s British coach but a practical way of coping with the luggage of the 47 passengers the coach could carry. *Stewart J. Brown*

1978 Reliance

Once production of the Swift had ended, in 1975, any operator wanting an AEC bus had but one choice – the Reliance. Hutchison of Overtown was a long-standing AEC customer and bought Reliance buses right up to the end, the last entering service in 1980, after which the company standardised on Volvos. Between 1977 and 1980 Hutchison took 11 Duple Dominant-bodied Reliances, one of which is seen leaving Wishaw for Larkhall in December 1978. *Stewart J. Brown*

1978 Reliance
Smiths of Wigan was a leading tour operator in the 1970s, and its new-vehicle intake for 1978 included ten Reliances with 53-seat Duple Dominant II bodies. By 1986 this coach was operating on contract to National Express, being seen in London in the ownership of Carlton Co-op Coaches of Nottingham. *Stewart J. Brown*

1979 Reliance
Yelloway of Rochdale was a staunch supporter of AEC in the 1960s and 1970s, during which
time it bought over 100 Reliances. Its last were five with 49-seat Plaxton Supreme IV bodywork,
and these entered service in 1979. One took part in that year's Blackpool Coach Rally. In 1980
Yelloway would buy Leyland Leopards. *Stewart J. Brown*

1979 Reliance
From the early 1970s Van Hool became an increasingly important supplier to UK coach operators, most commonly on Volvo chassis. A small number of Reliances were fitted with Van Hool bodies, and among the last were three delivered to Limebourne of London in 1979. This one is seen when new at the Blackpool Coach Rally. *Stewart J. Brown*

1979 Reliance
AECs had long figured on the Green Line network, although they were generally what might
be described as superior buses rather than proper coaches. That changed in 1977, when Green
Line operator London Country started running AEC Reliances with bodies by Duple and Plaxton.
It built up a fleet of 150, the last 90 being delivered in 1979 and including this coach with Duple
Dominant II body. *Stewart J. Brown*

1984 (1973) Reliance
Production of Reliances had ended by the time the registration system switched from numbers with year suffixes to year prefixes. However in 1983/4 ten East Kent Reliances were rebodied by Berkhof and appeared with new A-prefix Essex registrations, reflecting the involvement of Berkhof importer Ensignbus, based at Purfleet. The chassis had been new in 1973, with Duple Dominant bodywork. *Stewart J. Brown*

Postscript
For most of the period covered by this book the fleet of Yelloway of Rochdale was made up largely of AEC Reliances. Indeed, the company stopped buying them only when AEC stopped producing them. Three different styles of Plaxton body are visible on this line-up outside the company's Rochdale depot in 1980. *Gavin Booth*